APPLES

BY GAIL GIBBONS

HOLIDAY HOUSE · New York

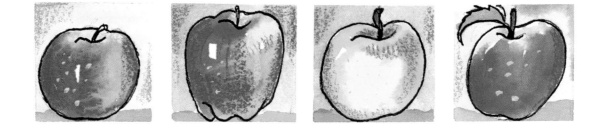

To Vicki and Dennis Schooley

Special thanks to Bob Welch
of Shearer's Greenhouses,
Bradford, Vermont

Copyright © 2000 by Gail Gibbons
All rights reserved
Printed and Bound in October 2019 at Phoenix Color, Hagerstown, MD, USA

22   24   25   23   21

Library of Congress Cataloging-in-Publication Data
Gibbons, Gail.
Apples / Gail Gibbons.—1st ed.
p.   cm.
Summary: Explains how apples were brought to America,
how they grow, their traditional uses and cultural significance,
and some of the varieties grown.
ISBN 0-8234-1497-3
1. Apples—Juvenile literature. [1. Apples.]   I. Title.
SB363.G53 2000
634'.11—dc21   99-054246
ISBN 0-8234-1669-0 (pbk.)

ISBN-13: 978-0-8234-1497-0 (hardcover)   ISBN-10: 0-8234-1497-3 (hardcover)
ISBN-13: 978-0-8234-1669-1 (paperback)   ISBN-10: 0-8234-1669-0(paperback)

An apple is a fruit. It grows on an apple tree. Apple trees grow in more parts of the world than any other fruit tree. They have been in existence for about two million years.

A
SEEDLING
is a very
young,
small tree.

The first American colonists brought apple seeds and seedlings with them from England.

As the colonists moved westward, they brought apple seeds and seedlings with them. Some settlers found that Native American Indians had already brought apple seeds west and had apple trees growing near their villages.

Many times during the early 1800s, John Chapman traveled throughout the wilderness of Ohio, Pennsylvania and Indiana planting apple seeds. Also, he gave seeds and seedlings to the settlers there. He became known as Johnny Appleseed.

Some apples are grown at home, but most are grown commercially.

A group of apple trees is called an APPLE ORCHARD.

Each year, about 250 million bushels of apples are grown in the United States, and about 28 million bushels are grown in Canada.

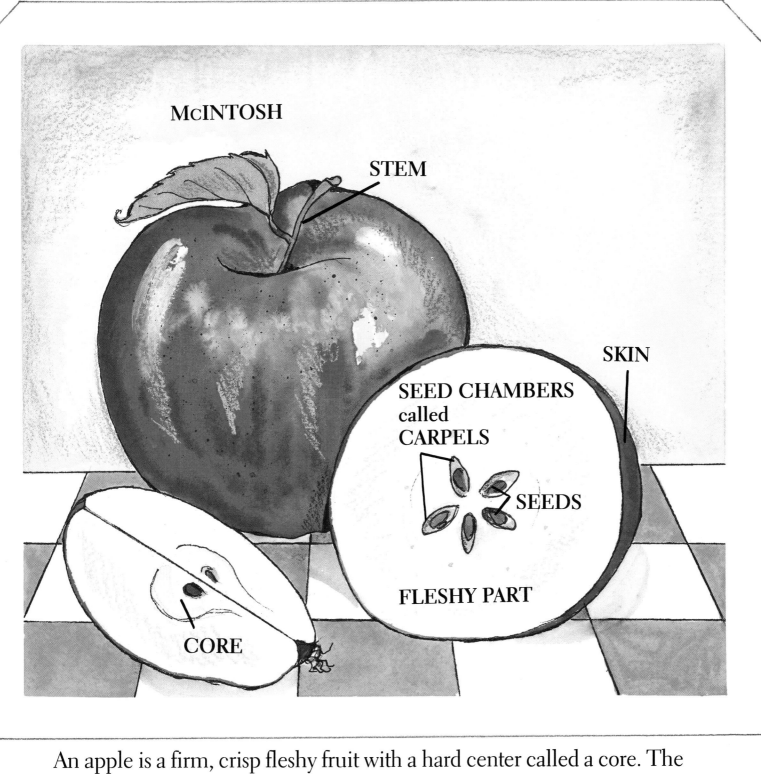

MᴄINTOSH

STEM

SKIN

SEED CHAMBERS
called
CARPELS

SEEDS

FLESHY PART

CORE

An apple is a firm, crisp fleshy fruit with a hard center called a core. The core has five seed chambers.

In the springtime, flowers called apple blossoms begin to bloom on the apple trees.

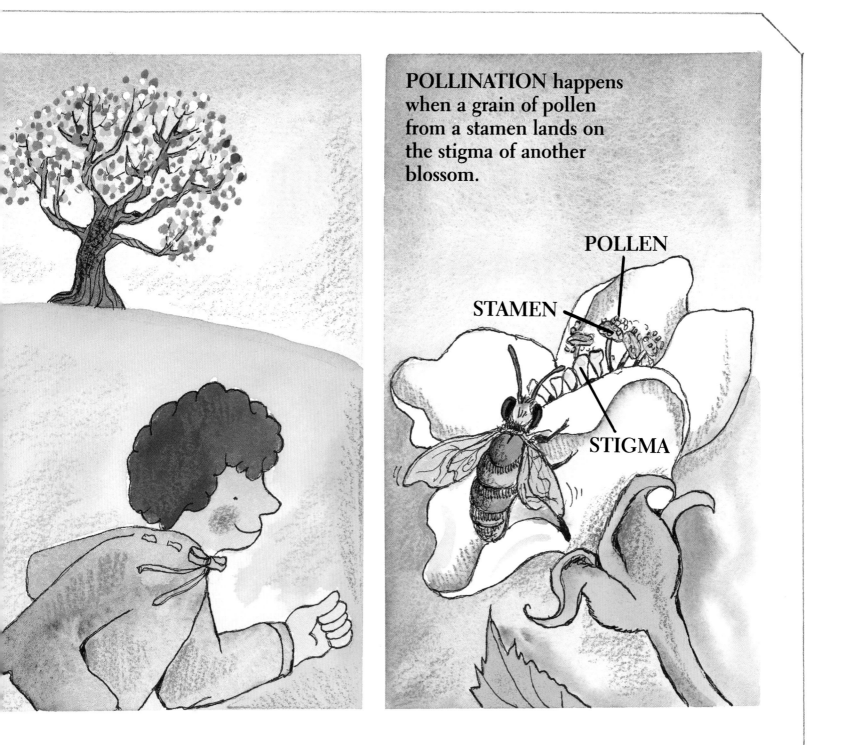

POLLINATION happens when a grain of pollen from a stamen lands on the stigma of another blossom.

POLLEN

STAMEN

STIGMA

Each blossom has to be pollinated in order for an apple to grow. The blossoms are usually pollinated by insects or by the wind.

After a while the blossoms begin to die and apples start to grow.

Throughout the warm summer the little apples grow bigger and bigger.

GOLDEN DELICIOUS

During the late summer or early fall the apples ripen.

When the trees are loaded with ripe apples, it is harvest time. Workers pick the apples by hand.

Some are shipped to stores. Some are used to make apple juice, apple cider, apple jelly, applesauce and lots of other apple products.

Some are sold in baskets at roadside stands.

During the fall, it is fun to go apple picking.

Also, there are country fairs. Awards are given to the best looking apples, the best tasting apple pies and the most delicious applesauce. There is apple cider, too.

During Halloween, there are caramel apples and candy apples.

Some people bob for apples.

DORMANT means alive but not actively growing.

When winter arrives, the apple tree branches become bare. The trees will become dormant until the next spring…

when the trees will produce a new crop of apples!

ROME BEAUTY

McINTOSH

RED DELICIOUS

GOLDEN DELICIOUS

Apples have many tastes, ranging from sweet to tart.

JONATHAN

STAYMAN

YORK

GRANNY SMITH

All apples are different shades of yellow, green and red, or a mix of those colors.

HOW TO PLANT AND CARE FOR AN APPLE TREE

1. It is best to plant a seedling in the fall.

2. Dig a hole that is big enough to give the seedling's roots room to grow.

3. After placing the seedling into the hole, add topsoil.

4. Pack down the soil to give the seedling support.

5. Water the seedling. It will need about ten gallons of water each week during the first few months after planting.

An apple tree will not grow apples until it is about five to eight years old. Each spring the tree branches are trimmed. This is called pruning.

Most apple trees grow to be about 20 feet (6m) tall. The soil around the trees should be fertilized. The pruning and fertilizing help produce lots of good apples.

AN APPLE A DAY...

1. Place dough for the bottom crust into a pie pan and trim off the edges.

2. Peel and slice six to eight apples. Granny Smiths and Jonathans are good to use for apple pies, because they are tart and stay firm when they are baked. Remove the cores. Put the slices into the pie pan.

3. Mix ½ cup (118 ml) brown sugar, ¼ teaspoon (1.23 ml) salt, ½ teaspoon (2.46 ml) cinnamon and ¼ teaspoon (1.23 ml) nutmeg. Sprinkle mixture over the apples.

4. Put a layer of dough on top. Pinch down the edges and remove any extra dough. Poke little holes in the top.

5. Bake for 50 minutes at 425°F (228°C).

Make your own apple pie with the help of an adult.

1. The apples are dropped into the hopper where they are cut up.

PRESS SCREW HANDLE

BLADES

HOPPER

2. The apple pieces drop into the tub until it is three-quarters full.

3. The press handle is turned and the apple pieces are squeezed, forcing cider through a cloth filter.

TUB **TRAY** **FILTER**

4. Apple cider flows into the tray and then runs into a container.

Here's how an apple cider press works.

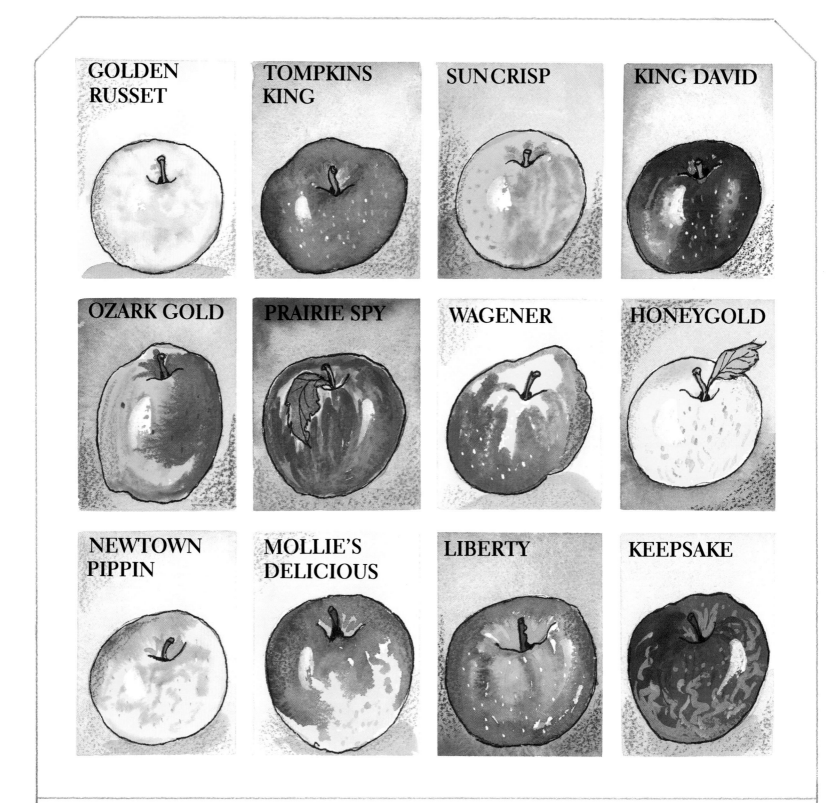

There are thousands of varieties, or kinds, of apples.

They are nutritious and delicious.

APPLES...APPLES...APPLES...

The smallest apples are crab apples, they make good apple jelly.

The most popular apple in the United States is the Red Delicious, which originated on a farm in Iowa about 1881.

The states of Washington, New York, Michigan, Pennsylvania and California produce the most apples in the United States.

Johnny Appleseed was born in Leominster, Massachusetts, and died in Ft. Wayne, Indiana.

Some people say when they like someone, "You're the apple of my eye!"

One apple, the Arkansas Black, is reddish purple and becomes nearly black by the end of the season.

The apple blossom is the state flower of Arkansas and Michigan.

There are over 7500 varieties of apples grown world wide and 2500 varieties grown in the United States.

If you store your apples in a cool and dry place, they can last for months.

The McIntosh apple was introduced in 1870 in Ontario, Canada. A monument marks the site of the first tree. Also, the Canadian provinces that grow the most apples are British Columbia, New Brunswick, Nova Scotia, Ontario and Quebec.